**DK READERS**

BEGINNING
1
TO READ

# Truck Trouble

BE-16-88

Written by Angela Royston

DK Publishing, Inc.

John got up very early
to make a special delivery.
He climbed up two steps
into his big blue truck.

John looked at the map.
Today was no day to get lost!
Then he started the truck,
checked the mirrors, and set off.

mirror

At a service station,
John checked the engine.
It needed some oil.
Then he filled up the fuel tank.

fuel tank

He looked at
the shiny engine.
"Don't let me down!"
he said.
"I can't be late!"

Next he had to pick up the cargo.
A forklift raised big boxes
into the back of John's truck.

There were also some small boxes marked "Special Delivery." John put these in the truck too.

John was in a hurry,
but he was also
very hungry.

He pulled into a truck stop
for breakfast.

John's friend Paul arrived
in his milk tanker.
He joined John for breakfast.

But John couldn't stop for long.
He had deliveries to make!

John drove on to the freeway.
It was jammed with traffic.
Cars and trucks beeped their horns.

John had to deliver the big boxes
to a nearby factory.
He left the freeway at the next exit.

John waved to the workers as he drove into the factory.

The workers helped him
unload the big boxes.

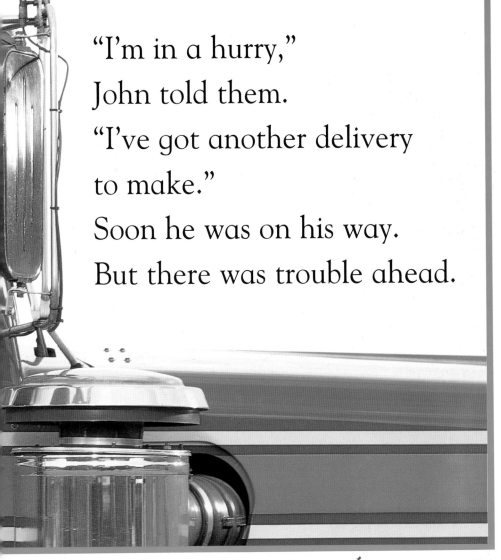

"I'm in a hurry,"
John told them.
"I've got another delivery
to make."
Soon he was on his way.
But there was trouble ahead.

A van had broken down!
John slammed on his brakes.
His truck screeched to a halt.

The road was very narrow.
John's truck was too wide
to get past the van.

John used his radio to call for help.
He also warned all other drivers
to stay away from that road.

Soon John saw flashing lights.
It was a tow truck!
The tow truck
towed the van
to a garage.

flashing lights

When the road was clear
John hurried on his way.
But there was more trouble ahead!

Boom! Boom!
John drove into a thunderstorm.
Rain began to pour down.

John turned on
the windshield wipers.

wiper

He drove very slowly.
"This isn't my day!"
he groaned.

John drove on and on.
Finally the rain stopped.
He pulled over to eat his lunch.

Then he rested
on a bunk
in the back of the cab.
He fell fast asleep!

cab

When he woke up, John thought,
"Now I'm in trouble!"

BANG!
"Oh no! A flat tire!"
John grabbed
his tools and
the spare wheel.

wheel

He unscrewed
the bolts and
took off the wheel.

bolt

Then he put on the spare.
It was hard work!

27

John drove into town.
He had to wait for
the traffic light
to turn green.

traffic
light

BE-16-88

"Hurry up!" thought John.
He was almost late
for his special delivery.

At last John arrived.
There was no time to spare!
He unloaded the boxes marked
"Special Delivery."

John was just in time for the party at the new children's hospital.

Inside the special boxes
were piles of toys.
"Thank you!" shouted the children.
"It was no trouble!" said John.

# Picture Word List

mirror

page 7

cab

page 24

fuel tank

page 9

wheel

page 26

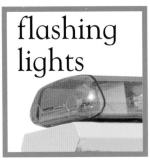
flashing lights

page 21

bolt

page 26

wiper

page 23

traffic light

page 28